YOUR KNOWLEDGE HAS VALUE

- We will publish your bachelor's and master's thesis, essays and papers

- Your own eBook and book - sold worldwide in all relevant shops

- Earn money with each sale

Upload your text at www.GRIN.com and publish for free

GRIN ☺

Model Structure for Block Chain Technology and Cryptocurrency for the Financial Services Sector in Zimbabwe

Gabriel Kabanda

Bibliographic information published by the German National Library:

The German National Library lists this publication in the National Bibliography; detailed bibliographic data are available on the Internet at http://dnb.dnb.de.

ISBN: 9783346486547
This book is also available as an ebook.

Print and binding: Books on Demand GmbH, Norderstedt, Germany
Printed on acid-free paper from responsible sources.

The present work has been carefully prepared. Nevertheless, authors and publishers do not incur liability for the correctness of information, notes, links and advice as well as any printing errors.

GRIN web shop: https://www.grin.com/document/1119788

Model Structure for Block Chain Technology and Cryptocurrency for the financial services sector in Zimbabwe

Professor Gabriel Kabanda
Secretary General
Zimbabwe Academy of Sciences, TREP Building, University of Zimbabwe
Harare, ZIMBABWE

ABSTRACT

The study was purposed to develop the model structure for blockchain technology and cryptocurrency, and determine the factors that influence the adoption of blockchain technology and cryptocurrency in Zimbabwe in order to make value-adding contributions to the cybersecurity risk management of the financial services sector. Cybersecurity is the collection of policies, techniques, technologies, and processes that work together to protect the confidentiality, integrity, and availability of computing resources, networks, software, programs, and data from attack. Cybersecurity threats have thus shifted from the cryptocurrency to attacking platforms using the cryptocurrency such as crypto exchanges. Essentially, there would be no bitcoin without Blockchain but Blockchain exists without bitcoin.the entire system works with a distributed ledger technology that operates on a decentralized pattern. The blockchain is distributed and highly available, exhibits irreversibility and immutability, and eliminates intermediaries in banking sector. For the blockchain to function fully, it requires components such as the Node, Transaction, Block as a data structure, Chain of the blocks, Miners to perform the block verification process, and Consensus (consensus protocol).

The Mixed Method methodology was used. The research utilized focus groups and document analysis to gather knowledge on the subject. A survey was conducted which included distribution of questionnaires and conducting interviews with heads of the banking sector. Findings suggest that, cryptocurrency which is based on blockchain technology is resistant to cybersecurity threats. The research also revealed that Zimbabwe has not yet legally adopted the use of cryptocurrency. We also concluded that cybersecurity systems in Zimbabwe are still under development and a lot of work has to done to ensure that the country is satisfactorily protected from cybersecurity threats. Since locally Bitcoin has been banned most of the traders have resorted to using South African accounts. Central Bank Digital Currency (CBDC) is another form of fiat money, similar to coin and banknote, which can be effectively exchanged for cash in denominations. The network layer is a bridge between the top regulators and ordinary users.the local distributed structure can utilize blockchain to solve the centralized load problem, enrich the financial organization structure, and expedite the payment delivery. Using block-chain technology, settlements can be increasingly optimized reducing the amount of time and money needed. They can allow auditors and government official's access to the block-chain. Transparency greatly increases by using smart contracts and block-chain technology.

Key Words: *Cybersecurity, Blockchain Technology, Cryptography, Cryptocurrency, Bitcoin, Cryptojacking.*

1.0 Introduction

1.1. Background

Cybersecurity is the protection of internet-connected systems such as hardware, software, and data from cyber-threats (Kshetri, N., 2017). Cybersecurity is the collection of policies, techniques, technologies, and processes that work together to protect the confidentiality, integrity, and availability of computing resources, networks, software, programs, and data from attack (Berman, D.S. *et al*, 2019). Cybersecurity can also be defined as protecting systems, networks, and programs from digital attacks. Cybersecurity takes many different forms, which include phishing and social engineering, ransomware and internet of things suspectibilty. Of primary concern is cryptojacking and the susceptibility of internet of things to cyberattacks. Due to the rapid increase in the use of the internet and internet of things, there is need to ensure that all the transactions and information on the internet is secure. The global acceptance and usage of cyptocurrency, raises a lot of cybersecurity uncertainties. Bitcoin is the most common type of cryptocurrency and it has enjoyed overwhelming success since its launch in 2008. Cryptocurrency is being equated to gold hence in some circles it is known as "digital gold." Zimbabwe like many other nations, slowly joined the whole world in using digital currency. The benefits of utilizing cybersecurity includes:
- ❖ Business protection against ransomware, malware, phishing, and social engineering.
- ❖ Protection for data and networks.
- ❖ Prevention of unauthorized users.
- ❖ Improves recovery time after a breach.
- ❖ Protection for end-users.
- ❖ Improvement of confidence in the product for both developers and customers.

Blockchain technology is the most important technological innovation in the banking sector. Zimbabwe has been battling with currency issues for over two decades. The situation reached its climax in 2008 when there was a total crush of the Zimbabwean Dollar. Since then, a number of currency regimes have been introduced to rescue our monetary situation, the most popular being the multi-currency regime. However, the regime could not last for a while because the exports became more expensive and thus less competitive on the market. Gradually, the market dried up of the most dominant currency of the regime (the US Dollar). Bonds notes were introduced also to cover the liquidity gap, but the Gresham's law which states that bad money drives out good money came to play and worsened the situation. However de-dollarization has not been that easy since its inception in 2019. There has been gross money creation in the mobile money platforms like Eco-cash, Tele-cash and One-money. The resultant effects were a hyper-inflation, unstable interest rates and an unstable foreign exchange rate. This however has been temporarily dealt with when the Central Bank banned some other transactions through these mobile money platforms. The purpose of this paper is to develop a model for blockchain technology and cryptocurrency and ascertain how the framework addresses cyber risks and creates value.

Blockchain as a digital, immutable, distributed ledger that chronologically records transactions in near real time (Shan, J., 2018). Nyagumbo, S. (2019) defined blockchain technology as a "block" of information linked together in an immutable, digitally distributed ledger through a process known as method hashing (Nyagumbo, S., 2019). According to Schutzer, D. (2016), blockchain technology is capable of providing an adequate and strong cybersecurity solution and an excellent privacy protection. Blockchain is a datastructure and

Distributed Ledger Technology (DLT), which uses decentralization and cryptographic hashing on the transparent and unalterable digital asset. Bailis and Song (2017) defines blockchain as a technology that provides a distributed ledger of transactions on a network that is scalable, secure, tamper-proof and accessible by each peer on the network. It is shared transactions, distributed over a network of members, made up of series of data blocks, each by itself contains a set of transactions. Cryptography is used to chain the blocks together and lock them to establish a public record of every transaction. The more blocks there are, the less the probability that blocks can be altered (Subramanian, R. and Chino, T., 2016). At this point, it is important to elaborate on the relationship between bitcoin and blockchain technology where, bitcoin is an electronic cryptocurrency that can be used to purchase goods and services based on incentivizing the participant miners, to validate the transactions and to render the network as stable as possible. Blockchain is the underlying technology that enables the Bitcoin network to operate in an open, autonomous, decentralized model where trust is enforced through cryptography and not over participants. Essentially, there would be no bitcoin without Blockchain but Blockchain exists without bitcoin (Tymoigne, 2015).

Fraud can be detected in real time in blockchain technology. Because the blockchain keeps records of each transaction, it allows banks to evaluate data for trends in real time. Blockchain and big data allow the security of banking transactions to be maximized. Kshetri, N. (2017) highlighted that the blockchain technology is a not a new introduction to the cyber world since its conceptualization in 1991 but recently gained popularity worldwide following the launch of bitcoin as the cyber currency on its platform. The blockchain technology is simply a melting pot whereby transactions are put in form of a puzzle. Users need to agree on a transaction; by making sure that each cryptographic harsh aligns.The entire system works with a distributed ledger technology that operates on a decentralized pattern.

Cryptocurrencies are a subset of digital currencies, which may either have decentralized institutions or are based on a decentralized network. Cryptocurrency derives its name from two things, *crypto* which refers to the technology and the base used to establish the currency which is *cryptography* and reference to the usage part which is the currency. Bryans (2014) defines a cryptocurrency as a digital token produced by cryptographic algorithms. The original cryptocurrency is bitcoin which was introduced in Japan by Satoshi Nakomoto (2008). It was launched as a decentralized electronic payment system, a peer to peer version of electronic cash without intermediaries, constructed with a cryptographic system that enables it to protect the information through a cipher, the encrypted unreadable format. The message can only be deciphered into plain text by the recipient who possess a secret key. Globally, Bitcoin is the most popular cryptocurrency as it represents 54% of the total market capitalization. In Zimbabwe, Bitmari is the most common type of bitcoin.

The history of blockchain technology is as highlighted in the diagram below on Figure 1 (Atlam, H. and Wills, G., 2018).

Figure 1: History of Blockchain Technology (**Adopted from** Atlam, H. and Wills, G. (2018))

3

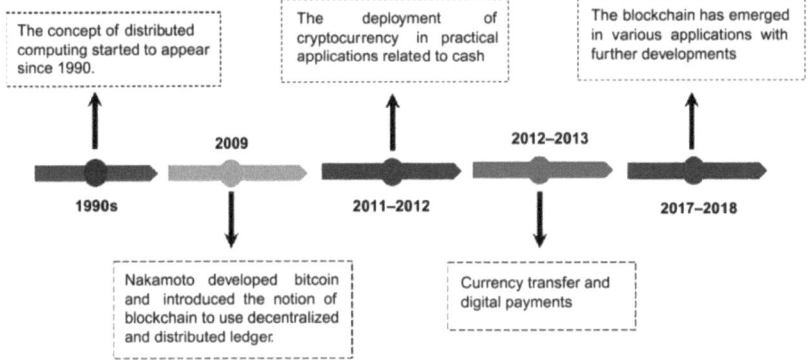

1.2 Statement of the Problem

Bitcoin is based on blockchain technology that is intended to promote a trust of mechanism in a peer-to-peer network based on the consensus of the majority of nodes. In order to verify a transaction in a cryptocurrency network, a proof of work is demanded from the node that verifies the transaction. The node has to do some heavy computations to prove that they are valid members of the network. Cryptocurrencies are digital currencies. The mere fact that the currency is decentralized and completely digitalized subjects it to the threat of cyberattacks. Cryptocurrency was developed on cyptography which has so far proved to be resistant to cyberattacks. Further, more types of cryptocurrencies are being developed, this subjects the whole world of cryptocurrencies to the risk of cyberattacks. With continuous development of cryptocurrencies and continuous development of cyberattacks, one wonders for how long cryptography will be able to withstand cyberattacks particularly in Zimbabwe where cybersecurity is still in its infancy stages.

The advent of IoT has brought about the need for a secure way of performing transactions on the internet without going thorough cumbersome processes. The use of the decentralised ledger with multistage cryptography provides a solution to the problem being faced by the Zimbabwean community at large.

1.3 Research Objectives

The objectives of the research are to:
a) Evaluate the performance of cryptocurrency and blockchain technology on a Zimbabwean cybersecurity system.
b) Ascertain the relationship between blockchain technology and cryptocurrency.
c) Assess the impact of blockchain technology and cryptocurrency on service delivery.
d) Determine the factors that influence the adoption of blockchain technology in Zimbabwe.

1.4 Research Questions

The research questions were to:

a. How do you rate the performance of blockchain technology and cryptocurrency on a Zimbabwean cybersecurity system?
b. What is the relationship between blockchain technology and cryptocurrency?
c. What is the impact of blockchain technology and cryptocurrency on service delivery?
d. Which factors influence the adoption of blockchain technology in Zimbabwe?

1.5 Significance of the Study

This research can be of considerable importance for companies in the banking sector as it alludes to the important aspects of emerging technology. The majority of banks are migrating to digital banking. This means they need to understand and understand how blockchain and big data analytics can help improve service delivery by banks.

Not only can banks benefit from this, regulators and law enforcement agencies can also use these technologies to enforce regulatory compliance by banking institutions because information can be securely accessed at the push of a button.

2.0 Review of the Literature

Trends in Blockchain and Cryptocurrency

The main issues on the adoption of cryptocurrencies centres on an early track record of liquidity, high volatility and potentially nebulous uses, Harvey, C. (2015). The most difficult part has been the classification of cryptocurrencies as whether they are digital or virtual currencies and how their value should be determined. There has been an increase in virtual currencies globally. These include Facebook credits, Microsoft Pints and Amazon Coins. Harvey, C. (2015) elaborated that, unlike Bitcoins these currencies are issued by blue chip companies and are not linked to any claims on real assets. For instance if a large company launches a currency to compete with traditional currencies, network effects could ensure that the currency is taken-up quite quickly by members of the network. Wagner, A. (2014) postulates that the value and distribution of virtual currencies are typically controlled by a centralized authority, which in most cases is the issuing authority and they are used specifically to process online transactions.

Another significant argument has been the issue of whether cryptocurrency should be considered to be digital currency or digital assets. Given the background already explored, one would expect to view the token as a currency but Glaser, F. et al. (2014) argues that users of cryptocurrency are not interested in an alternate transaction system but seek to participate in an alternative investment vehicle. In America, the US Inland Revenue Services recognizes cryptocurrency as a virtual currency and therefore it should be considered to be an asset (Drawbaugh, K., and Temple-West, P., 2014). Other early adopters such as Norway, Sweden and Canada also recognize cryptocurrency as an asset. Germany which is also an early adopter accepts that cryptocurrency is a unit of account to be used for trading and taxation purposes within the country in the form of "private money" (Clinch, M., 2013). There has been no global unanimity on the recognition of cryptocurrency but distinctions have been made on a jurisdiction bases basing on the capacity to monitor and regulate it.

Virtual currencies are associated with five potential risks which are of interest to central banks and these are price stability, financial stability, payment system stability, lack of regulation and reputation (ECB, 2012). Virtual currencies could make the goal of price stability somewhat difficult if they are not primarily controlled by the central banks through fiscal and monetary policy. The reduced control over money supply can also impact on financial stability through the central bank's ability to intervene in the foreign exchange rate market. However, speculation with respect to the virtual currency may occur due to the history of cyberattacks. The value of virtual currencies depends largely on whether or not a second party is willing to accept the unit as a means of final payment, hence there is no guarantee of payment (ECB, 2012). There is no clear definition of the rights and obligations of each party, since there is no legal basis for virtual currencies.

The Bitcoin network of nodes is not maintained by a single entity in a single country but there are more than 7,000 reachable nodes spread over 100 countries. Bitcoin's biggest innovations are the absence of central entity or authority, which minimizes single point of failure, and distributed ledger which provides immutability to reduce fraud and hacking (Mims, C., 2018). The system is essentially "trustless". Users can trust the system of the public ledger stored worldwide on many different decentralized nodes as opposed to having to establish and maintain trust with third party intermediary. The blockchain technology as an electronic wallet provides pseudo anonymity as it is created from the user's private and public key which do not not require personally identifiable information to be encoded in a transaction. Bitcoin exchanges and electronic wallets have been hacked many times but not the underlying blockchain. It is virtually possible to hack the underlying blockchain but that would require tremendous computing resources such no individual has or a government entity might possess (Fahad, S., 2018). Ownership of Bitcoins can be transferred, over peer-to-peer network and they can be purchased, sold, and exchanged for other currencies at Bitcoin exchanges such as Coinbase and Kraken. In 2013 there was an increase in the transactions that were being processed over Silk Road with Bitcoin being the preferred currency. Silk Road was a platform for anonymously buying and selling illegal drugs and guns and the Federal Bureau of Investigations in the United States of America ended closing Silk Road (Wikipedia, 2018). In global news Bitcoin had already made headlines because it was being associated with the dark market. Bitcoin has continued to grow in popularity with its lower transaction costs and absence of third party institutions, despite the bad publicity, especially in international money transfer, small businesses and among the unbanked population. Investors are also speculating on Bitcoins by holding them with hopes that their intrinsic value will increase (Joon, I., 2018).

Cryptojacking is the unauthorized use of a device's resources to mine cryptocurrencies (European Union Agency for Cybersecurity, 2020). In simple terms it is the theft of a company's computing power. Targets includes any connected device, such as computers and mobile phones. Cryptojacking is one of the greatest, consistent and renewable persistent threats in the cryptocurrency and blockchain technology era. Recent trends in cyberattacks has shifted as more malware code writers are improving on their malware to include cryptojacking and crytomining capability to their methodologies. The new generation of malware is using cryptojacking code to hunt for digital crypto wallet addresses and target specific machines/devices and crypto victims. Chiu, J., et al (2017) argues that cryptojacking has become a profitable business since the threat and sophistication of malware based mining has increased and that clearly shows that the interest has shifted into mining cryptocurrency. The developers and designers of new cryptocurrency have identified the possibility of utilizing Application Specific Intergrated Circuit (ASIC), to mine. Measures have also been taken to make sure that mining can be done on a personal computer, rather than detected machines, therefore the new generation of cryptocurrency is ASAIC resistance, therefore subsequent miners of such crypto will have to do it on a regular PC, which has unintentionally allowed the spread of malicious mining malware and now all standard PC around the globe has become a target for crypto jacking and malware mining.

Blockchain technology is normally used with cryptocurrencies such as Bitcoin. It is a database of records of transactions that is distributed and validated and managed by a computer network around the world. Instead of a single central authority like a bank, the records are overseen by a large community and no single person is in control and no one can go back and change or delete a transaction history (Manyenyere, J., 2020). Blockchain technology is considered one of the most dynamic technologies in the financial market and enables the creation of decentralized currencies. Execution of digital contracts and intelligent assets that can be controlled via the Internet. Recent research on blockchain has mainly focused on financial transactions and distributed ledger systems. The blockchain technology uses the shared data infrastructure which updates is in real time and transactions can be processed in seconds with sophisticated calculations.

The advantages of using blockchain technology in the banking sector are as follows (Jani, S., 2018):

❖ *Near real-time:* Blockchain enables the real-time processing of recorded transactions, the elimination of friction losses and the reduction of risks.

❖ *No intermediary:* With the decentralization of the blockchain, anyone around the world can send transactions to peers without a third party. Blockchain technology is based on cryptographic proof rather than trust, so that two parties can do business directly with one another without the need for a trusted third party.

❖ *Distributed Ledger:* The distributed peer-to-peer network records a public transaction history. The blockchain is distributed and highly available. The blockchain usually does not preserve the identity of the parties or the transaction data, only proof of the existence of the transaction.

❖ *Irreversibility and Immutability:* The blockchain contains a specific and verifiable record of every single transaction ever made. This prevents previous blocks from being changed and, in turn, prevents duplicate spending, fraud, abuse and tampering with transactions.

❖ *Smart contracts:* The loans, leasing contracts, contracts of the entire banking industry can be integrated into smart contracts, which paves the way for conflict-free transactions. Stored procedures executed on a Blockchain to process predefined business steps and execute a legally enforceable / business transaction without the involvement of an intermediary.

Blockchain technology and the banking sector in Zimbabwe
Blockchain technology in Zimbabwe is still in its infancy stages, and adoption of this type of technology has been slow with some banks like Steward Bank adopting it. Zimbabwe's banking industry today faces issues such as rising operating costs, increasing susceptibility to fraudulent attacks on centralized servers, and challenges in ensuring transparency. All of this, primarily because most of Bank transactions, from customer account opening to globalization payments can require an intensive manual processing and documentation involve costly and

7

time-consuming intermediaries, as these transactions must be validated by multiple participants at various times, which causes the delay, resulting in a near lack of real-time, fraud-proof solution (Manyenyere, J., 2020).

Banks are continually exploring new ways to transact faster for better customer service, while ensuring cost efficiency in their operations and ensuring transparency for customers and regulators. For this, Blockchain potentially provides a solution for banks as inherently, it helps to eliminate intermediaries, maintains an immutable record of transactions and also facilitates the execution of transactions in real time. This could potentially reduce the costs of manual labour and lead to better service and customer satisfaction (Jani, S., 2018). Sharma, A.(2019) postulates that blockchain enables banking institutions to detect attempted fraud in real time. Because the blockchain contains records for every transaction, banks can examine data looking for patterns in real time.

Conceptual Framework

Tschorsch, F., and Scheuermann, B. (2016) postulate that blockchain technology cryptographically captures and stores a consistent, immutable, linear event log of transactions between networked actors in a fully distributed system. This distributed ledger technology is physically stored, updated, and validated by the parties involved in all the transactions within a network. In such a blockchain technology network, transparency is enforced and system-wide consensus on the validity of the transaction is guaranteed (Tschorsch, F., and Scheuermann,B., 2016). The current blockchain technology processes monetary transactions and ensures compliance of the transaction with programmable rules in the form of "smart contracts" all without a third party even with little trust among the parties. Beck, R., and Müller-Bloch, C. (2017) echoed that implementations differ regarding their mechanisms to enforce consensus, the power of included programming languages, their capabilities to define who can participate in a network, and the type of cryptocurrency they include.

The key features and uses of Blockchain are as follows:

A. Immutability

Immutability means something that cannot be changed or altered. Blockchain technology is a a permanent, unalterable network. Schutzer, D. (2016) argued that Blockchain technology works slightly different than the typical banking system. The blockchain does not depend on centralized authorities but uses a collection of nodes where each node on the system has a copy of the digital ledger and checks the validity of each transaction. The transaction is only added to the ledger if the majority agrees that it is valid. This promotes transparency and makes it corruption-proof. So, without the consent from most nodes, no one can add any transaction blocks to the ledger (Schutzer, D., 2016). Another fact, which backs up the list of key blockchain features is that, once the transaction blocks get added on the ledger, no one can just go back and change it. Thus, any user on the network will not be able to edit, delete or update it.

B. Decentralized

The network is decentralized, meaning it does not have any governing authority or a single person looking after the framework.The network is decentralized as a group of nodes maintains the network. Blockchain enables the users to store anything starting from cryptocurrencies, important documents, contracts, or other valuable digital assets.

B. Enhanced Security

In addition to decentralization, another layer of protection for users is provided by cryptography. Cryptography acts as a firewall for attacks besides being a complex mathematical algorithm. Kshetri, N. (2017) posit that every information on the blockchain is hashed cryptographically. In this way, the true nature of the data is hidden. A mathematical algorithm produces a different kind of value for each input data whilst maintaining a fixed length. Kshetri, N. (2017) further explained that you could think of it as a unique identification for every data. A unique hash is generated for each of the blocks in the ledger and each block contains the hash of the previous block. Hence, changing or trying to tamper with the data will mean changing all the hash IDs. Blockchain Security provides premium protection for enterprises (Kshetri, N., 2017). Hashing is quite complex, and it is impossible to alter or reverse it. No one can take a public key and produce a private key. The system does not tolerate slight changes as a single change in the input could lead to a completely different ID (https://101blockchains.com). Corruption of the network can only be achieved by altering every data stored on every node in the network. Its costly and not possible to access and hack millions of computers (https://101blockchains.com).

C. Distributed Ledgers

A public ledger usually provides every information about a transaction and the participant. There is transparency on the contents of the ledger as the ledger on the network is maintained by all other users on the system. This is the reason it is considered one of the blockchain essential features.

D. Consensus

According to Kshetri, N. (2017) every blockchain thrives because of the consensus algorithms. Every blockchain makes use of a consensus to help the network make decisions as a group of nodes active on the network as they agree quickly and faster on a matter. In a consenus, the majority wins and the minority must then support it, hence the network is thrustless. Consequently, every decision on the network is a winning scenario for the blockchain, which provides a high degree of fairness on the web (https://101blockchains.com).

Blockchain Architecture

Like conventional public ledger, a blockchain is a sequence of blocks which holds a complete list of transaction records and Figure 2 illustrates an example of a blockchain with the previous block hash contained in the block header. The genesis block is the founding block in a blockchain which has no parent block.

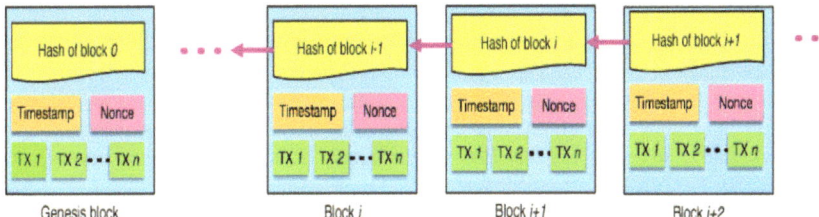

Figure 2 An example of Blockchain which consists of a continuous sequence (Hameed, B.I., 2020)

Block body

The block body consists of a transaction counter and transactions. The block size and size of each transaction determines the maximum number of transactions that a block can contain (Hameed, B. I.,2020). The figure below illustrates the block structure showing the header and body.

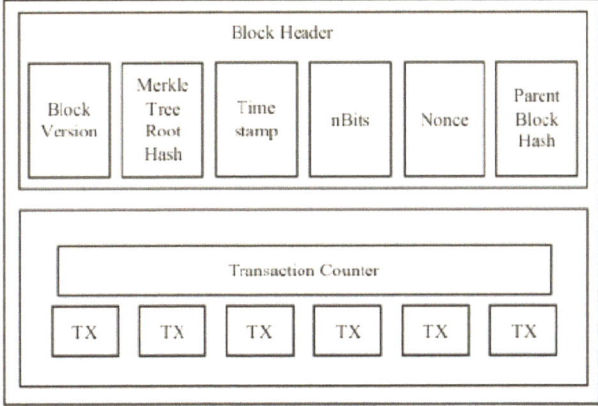

Figure 3 Block structure (Hameed, B. I., 2020)

How the Blockchain works

To add a block into the blockchain, the following criteria should be fulfilled first:

a) A transaction must be made as agreement between the users in order to initiate the addition of a new block into the block chain.

b) The transaction that is made must be verified and this verification is done by a computer network that comprise millions of computers (nodes) across the globe. This network validates the transaction details.

c) The transaction is to be stored in a block. Upon verification of the transaction and accuracy confirmed, the information is stored in the block with its unique hash. This block is then stored in the blockchain along with thousands of other blocks.

1

d) The last steps include the assignment of Hash. As soon as the block chain is hashed, it can be added in the blockchain.

The block as part of the blockchain is publicly accessible and can be viewed by everyone in the network. The copy of the blockchain is available to every user and the information accessible in relation to the transactions detail inclduing the date, time and amount added to the blockchain (Hameed, B. I.,2020). How the blockchain works is shown on Figure 4 below.

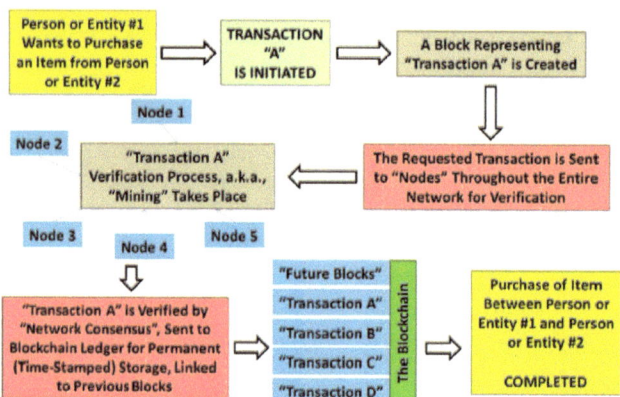

Figure 4: How blockchain work (Hameed, B. I., 2020)

Cryptocurrency
Cryptocurrency is an application of blockchain and a form of a digital currency. It basically provides it's uses with encrypted digital currency, which is independent of any centralized banking system, but rather it is a form of units or blocks (Hameed, B. I., 2020). Common examples of cryptocurrency include are Bitcoin (BTC), Ethereum (ETH), Ripple (XRP), etc.

The blockchain requires a public address to transact and send money. Nevertheless, many cryptocurrency wallets come with a QR code embedded in them so that the buyer can easily scan into their own wallet application to make a transfer instead of typing the encoded address when transacting.

The logic behind making a transaction is that the sender's wallet digitally signs the transaction with their private key and anyone knowing their public key (public address) can verify that they authorized the transaction. The transaction done within the blockchain network is then transmitted to one of the mining nodes. This node sends the information it has to other nodes and they do the same until every node in the network has a copy of the transaction. If a transaction is included in the block, details such as the addresses of the sender and receiver, amount, sender's signature are written into the data section of the block. During the process, a certain node also signs it with their private key (just as the sender did) to protect it from modification then send it to every node until everyone has a copy of the block.

1

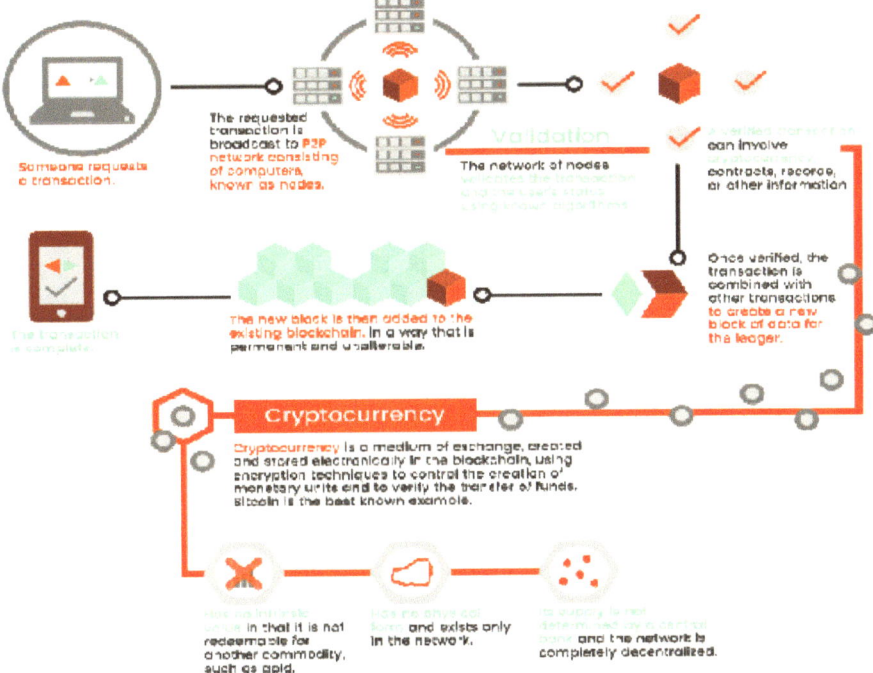

Figure 5: How the Cryptocurrency Transaction Works (Hameed, B. I., 2020)

How the Blockchain Technology framework addresses cyber risks and creates value

Cyber risk arises when there is exposure to harm or potential loss resulting from breaches of or attacks on information systems related to technical infrastructure or the use of technology within an organization (RSA, 2016). Below we explain how the Blockchain Technlogy Application framework addresses cyber risks and create value:

A. *Integrity*

Integrity is about providing information security and ensuring information non-repudiation and authenticity (Piscini, E., *et al.*, 2017). Data integrity is ensured in organizations through the provision of Blockchain's built in characteristics, immutability and traceability.

B. *Immutability*

Blockchain ledger is immutable as we focus on data integrity. For each transaction in a block, the sender cryptographically signs it, the miner cryptographically signs the block, every block provides a hash of the immediately preceding block, and a

1

consensus is reached by all the participants in the blockchain network pertaining to its truth. Altering a transaction in the blockchain would require the attacked to change each subsequent block, accordingly, and reverse the consensus decision arrived at by the majority of the network participants to adopt the new chain. Due to the hashing properties and computation power required, that situation is close-to-impossible, to achieve. Integrity is the greatest merit of blockchain because it is tamper-resistant (Kerkeni, L., *et al.*, 2016). Merkle trees are used in the hashing of blockchain technologies. Merkle tree summarizes all transactions in a block into a single fingerprin for verification of the authenticity of the transaction. The Merkle tree within a blockchain is illustrated below on Figure 6.

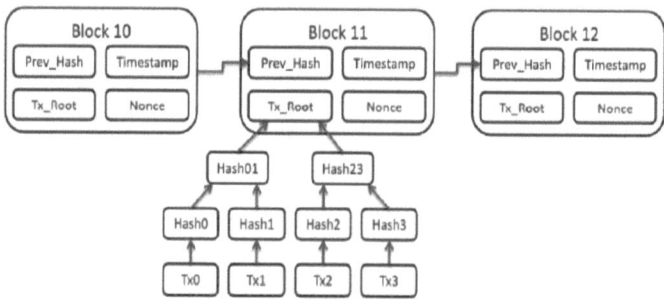

Figure 6: Merkle tree (Kerkeni, L., *et al.*, 2016)

C. Traceability

Traceability is supported by the timestamping and digital signing of the blockchain for every transaction added to a public or private blockchain. This important property is key for non repudiation purposes whcih provides assurance of non duplication of the authenticity of their signature on a file from the point of origin (Piscini, E., *et al.*, 2017).

D. Confidentiality

Sensitive information is not disclosed to unauthorized individuals, entities, or processes (Piscini, E., *et al.*, 2017).

E. Data access and disclosure

Information on the blockchain network cannot be read or retrieved by an attacker. Confidentiality of the data is effectively guaranteed by the full encryption of the data blocks (Piscini, E., *et al.*, 2017).

F. Privacy

Without loss of generality, public blockchain networks bind transactions to accounts. It is only the individual whose identity is anonymous and in possession of the corresponding private key who is able to launch a transaction on behalf of the account through a cryptographic signature (Kerkeni, L., *et al.*, 2016).

G. Availability

Provision of timely and reliable access ensures availability of the information.

1

H. No single point of failure

Because blockchains do not have a single point of failure and so its not possible to achieve an IP-based DDoS attack that can disrupt the normal operation. In the unlikely event of an attack on a node, the data will still be accessible via other nodes within the network (Piscini, E., *et al.*, 2017).

I. Operational resilience

The blockchain platfrom is operationally resilient due to the number of nodes of the peer to peer nature that operate in a distributed fashion 24/7. A node under attack can easily be made redundant in both public and private blockchain setups, and business operations will continue as usual (Piscini, E., *et al.*, 2017).

H. Backup and recovery

Blockchain technologies provide secure storage and automatic recovery procedures. The backup and recovery system ensures that changes to the files are simultaneously copied to the storage location. This facilitates automatic recovery with the most recent changes.

It is imperative to understand that the blockchain originated as the technology for bitcoin or cryptocurrency but has prevalently grown into a prospective mitigant technology for cybersecurity. A cryptocurrency is a digital asset intended to work as a medium of exchange in which distinct coin ownership records are stored in a ledger existing in a form of computerized database or blocks using strong cryptography to secure transaction records, to control the creation of additional coins, and to verify the transfer of coin ownership (Qin, R., et.al, 2018). With Bitcoin as a boundary, cryptocurrency can be alienated into two stages namely those represented by E-Cash and the decentralized cryptocurrencies based on blockchain (Qin, R., et.al, 2018). Nonetheless, the existence of blockchain technologies and cryptocurrency cannot supplant fiat money.

There is a massive fissure amongst decentralized cryptocurrency and central bank digital currency (CBDC) with respect to monetary governance and velocity of circulation in general. The Reserve Bank proposes the role and security requirements (functional requirements) for blockchain technology and cryptocurrency. A thorough and ample scrutiny of the typical cryptocurrency is provided for through the CBDC scheme. Blockchain mainly relies on three concepts which are:
  i.   Peer-to-peer network
  ii. Distributed Consensus
  iii. Public-key Cryptography.

Structure of Block-chain Technology Application Model

Block-chain technology is an underlying construct of Bit-coin, so no discussion of block-chain is practical without also touching on the bit-coin crypto currency (Sultan, K., *et al,* 2018). Nakamoto (2008) presented the strategy to overcome the double-spending scenario, a common problem with the previous crypto-currencies. The blockchain consists of a chain of hashed timestamps where the hash includes the previous timestamp of each current timestamp and the chain is reinforced behind it (Nakamoto, 2008). This strategy was later refined for Bitcoin and the concept still remains of using a chain of blocks which are each cryptographically linked to the previous using a hash digest. In this way, the blockchain becomes a sequence of records, each hashed and linked to the previous block, as illustrated by the structure defined by Nakamoto (2008) shown on Figure 7.

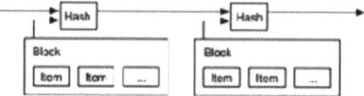

Figure 7: Nakamoto's Block-chain Proposal (Source: Nakamoto, 2008: p 2)

For the above block-chain proposal by Nakamoto (2008) to fully function, the structure should have the following six components:

- Node – This could be a user or computer within the blockchain architecture.
- Transaction – representing the smallest unit of the records and information set of the building block of the blockchain system
- Block – a data structure that keeps a record of the transactions distributed to the all nodes in the network.
- Chain – a sequence of the blocks in a specific order.
- Miners – specific nodes which perform the block verification process before adding to anything to the block-chain structure.
- Consensus (consensus protocol) – The blockchain operations are guided by a set of rules and arrangements agreed upon by the majority of the participants on the network.

Figure 8 depicts how these six components interact in a block-chain technology structure.

Editor's note: This image was removed due to copyright reasons

Figure 8: How Block-chain Technology Works (Source: https://mlsdev.com/blog/156-how-to-build-your-own-blockchain-architecture)

The interaction of these six components produces a strong block-chain technology network that has the following characteristics:

- ❖ Cryptography – block-chain transactions are validated and trustworthy due to the complex computations and cryptographic proof among involved parties
- ❖ Immutability - any records made in a block-chain cannot be changed or deleted
- ❖ Provenance - refers to the fact that it is possible to track the origin of every transaction inside the block-chain ledger
- ❖ Decentralization - each member of the block-chain structure has access to the whole distributed database. On the contrary, the consensus algorithm permits control of the network.
- ❖ Anonymity- each participant on the blockchain uses a generated address network and not the user identity.
- ❖ Transparency - the block-chain system cannot be corrupted. This is very unlikely to happen, as it requires huge computing power to overwrite the block-chain network completely.

3. Methodology

Coughlan, M., *et al* (2007) define research methodology as the nuts and bolts of how a research study is undertake. This means the step by step approach of the research. In this paper, a Mixed Approach Research (MAR) approach was adopted. Mixed Method Research is defined as a research method that employs two research methods simultaneously to create a research outcome stronger than either method individually (Kaushik, V., and Walsh, C., 2019). According to Kaushik, V.,and Walsh, C. (2019), the MAR has the following benefits hence it was adopted in this research as it provides:

- strengths that offset the weaknesses of both focus groups and document analysis. This was the rational used by the author in choosing the MAR.
- a more complete and comprehensive understanding of the research problem than either focus groups or document analysis alone.
- an approach that facilitates development of better, more context specific instruments.

A focus group is a qualitative data collection method where the chosen respondents meet and discuss the subject matter (Hancook, B., *et al* 2007). In theory focus groups looks more or less like interview but participants interact with each other and they critique and analyses each other's contribution which does happen in an ordinary interview. The researcher usually provides a guide on the topic so as not to lose focus on the subject under discussion as stated by Kitzinger, J. (1995). Focus groups are most ideal where there is a significant time and resource constraint and the interview wants to find out other people's understanding and experiences about the problem and reasons behind their line of thinking. In this case the focus group discussion was facilitated by the researcher who allowed the respondents to respond to open ended questions. The researcher also moderated on the discussion making sure that the most important parts of the discussion are covered.

Study Sample
Because of the limitations of a census, researchers can extract a sample from the population from which data is collected. Crawshaw, J., and Chambers, J. (2001) define a sample as a smaller set of data that a researcher chooses or selects from a larger population by using a pre-defined selection method. One major characteristic of a sample is that, it should be representative of the population. In this study, simple random sampling was used to come up with the sample that was used in this research. Random numbers were assigned to each population unit and the numbers were randomly picked from a basket. This entails that each population unit had an equal chance of being selected into the sample. The following formula was used to calculate the sample size:

$$n = \frac{N}{1 + Ne^2}$$

Where: *n= sample*
N= N=study population
e=level of significance chosen (in this case 15%)

Therefore:

$$n = \frac{100}{1 + 100(0.15)^2}$$

n= 30

The focus group was attended by 30 members and the meeting was done at the UZ Business School lecture room HLT200 on 13 December 2020 at 0900. Document analysis was also used to gather and an understanding on how cryptocurrency and blockchain technology. Document analysis is a method which involves the researcher analyses several documents to bring an interpretation and a voice around an assessment topic. Document analysis involves coding of contents into themes similar to how focus groups scripts are analyzed. In this case publications and research papers on cryptocurrency and blockchain technology were analyzed.

Research methodology

A qualitative research methodology was used. The research study draws on two major theoretical approaches: Discourse Theory (DT) by Laclau and Mouffe and Critical Discourse Analysis (CDA) by Fairclough. All discourse analytical approaches coincide at some point in their view the language and the subject.

Research Design

Research design as the "logical and methodical attitude to the assortment of data so that evidence can be found from the data" (Saunders, M., 2003). Blueprint detailing the means and processes that must be used to obtain the facts needed by the resolution maker to collect and analyse. The research design helps to obtain clear answers to a significant problem.

The researcher used the descriptive survey research design that takes into account individuals with deep correction. Give answers to; who, what, where, how and why study inquiries. Examine the circumstances or associations that occur, the opinions that are alleged, the procedures in which they work, the causes and effects that are evident.

The scholar used a descriptive survey research design because it was inexpensive, required no sophisticated skills, aided in the collection of original data, and also facilitated coverage of a broader population. Detailed analysis was performed and more comprehensive data was obtained through descriptive survey research design. This research design goes beyond the mere compilation and tabulation of facts and opinions about the current conditions of things.

Research instruments

A research instrument is defined as a tool that is used to collect the data necessary to find solutions to the problems under study. The researcher used questionnaires, interviews and data collection from observations.

Data collection procedures

Data collection procedures are the steps or activities that describe the general way the data will be collected. Data acquisition processes are phases in the control of the research instruments. As part of the data collection process, the researcher conducted a pilot study in which he initially distributed five (5) questionnaires and conducted five (5) interviews with the head of banking. Head of Risk and Compliance, Head of ICT, Managing Director and Chief Financial Officer of Success Microfinance Bank, who noted that some of the questions were not clear and needed to be changed for clarity.

The technique was used to determine the relationship between blockchain technology and big data.

A regression analysis model was used to determine the relationship between blockchain technology and big data analysis.

This section summaries the strategies and procedures that were used to collect and analyses data. The methodology focuses on the approach, design, sources of data, the study site and population, the sample size and sampling technique, the procedures of data collection, the data gathering tools, the methods of data analysis by which knowledge is gained giving the work plan of the research. The major areas that were of particular concern to the proper execution of this study included: study area and target population, the collection of primary and secondary data, and the data analysis techniques used in arriving at the solution to the problem under study.

The research onion below on Figure 9 shows the pictorial view of the route taken on this study from the philosophies, Approaches, Strategies, Choices, Time horizon and data collection and data analysis

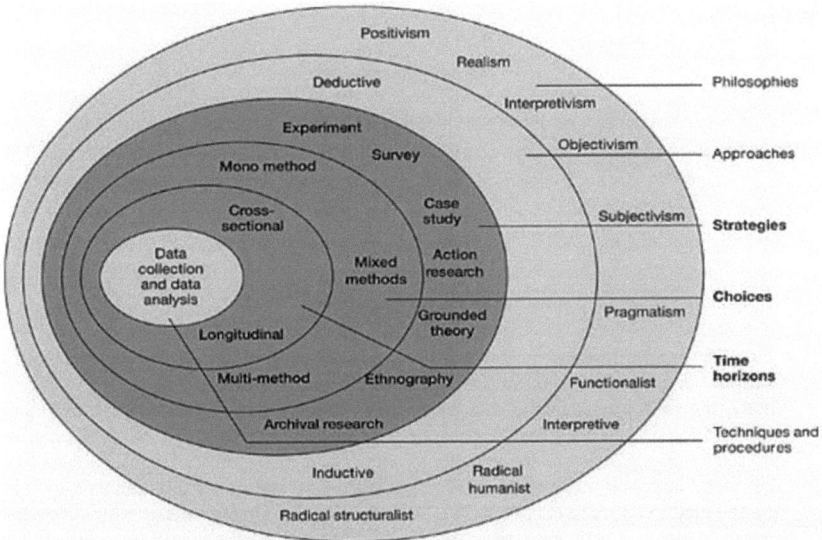

Figure 9: Research Onion
Source: (Cooke-Davies, T.J, 2010:109)

The study is an exploratory study because there is little information in Zimbabwe concerning the use case of block chain in the financial services sector. Therefore, the approach taken was the interpretivism approach to carry out a qualitative research since there is need for quality information on the subject area.

4. Data Analysis

In this episode of the study, the researcher presents, interprets, and analyses the key findings of this research. Earlier sections of the research formulated the basis for absolute interpretation along with the analysis of the results. The following topics are covered in this chapter: Research questions and determine whether the relationship between block chain technology and big data analysis in the banking sector can be successfully used to increase the efficiency of the way banks provide services to improve Zimbabwe.

Response Analysis

Position Held	Number of Questions	
	Answered	Not Answered
Managing Director	10	-
Finance Director	10	-
Head of Banking	10	-
Head of ICT	10	-
Head of Risk and Compliance	10	-

Figure 1: Responses

A total of 5 questionnaires, each with 10 identical questions, were sent to 5 managers of the Bank and a total of 5 questionnaires distributed giving an overall response rate of 100%. The results presented in Table 1 above show that the response rate from questionnaires and conducted personal interviews was high. Hence, this improved the authenticity and validity of the research. Kabanda, G. (2020) postulated that a response rate of 70% or more is very good if a research survey is conducted through questionnaires, hence the response rate in this study is 100%, which is more than satisfactory and, therefore feasible.

From the data gathered the researcher made the following observations on the performance of cryptocurrency and blockchain on Zimbabwean Cybersecurity System:
- ❖ Firstly, the randomness of the data transactions within blockchain's context, and their strong encryption, means that neither the blocks nor the chain can be duplicated or infiltrated using malware or other exploits.
- ❖ The most common cyberattacks on cryptocurrency and blockhain technology has targeted the 'nodes' or users rather than the actual blockchain technology which supports Bitcoin. Several attacks have been noted and examples of the significant ones are as follows: A ransomware attack on Taiwanese electronics giant Foxconn has resulted in hackers demanding US$34.7 million in Bitcoin. This is a very recent case of cyberattack which occurred on 29 November 2020.
- ❖ A significant proportion of cyberattacks are targeting crypto exchanges rather than the actual Bitcoin and evidence from the Group IB, Hi-tech Crime Trends 2018 report estimates that cryptocurrency exchanges suffered a total loss of US$882 million due to target attacks in 2017 and in the first three quarters of 2018. Group IB Experts reported of at least 14 crypto exchanges having been hacked. Five attacks have been linked to North Korean hackers from Lazarus state-sponsored group, including the infamous attack on Japanese crypto exchange Coincheck, when US$534 million in cryptocurrency was stolen.
- ❖ Cybersecurity for bitcoin may be difficult to mainatin as some white-collar criminals could take advantage of their peers' excitement about blockchain to commit entirely secure acts of fraud that might not be discovered for days, making bitcoin cyber security hard to maintain.

1

- The research also recognized a strong need for due diligence in choosing and keeping trading partners mainly because if business leaders use blockchain overzealously and don't conduct due diligence with potential clients or partners, they open themselves up to exploitation.
- The also recognized the importance of the role of the cybersecurity specialist as one of the most crucial positions in the modern business world, especially if a company is interested in innovative technologies.
- The research also emphasized on the need to engage in cyber insurance as a secondary measure to resuscitate the business after a cyberattack. Most companies seem to be of the opinion that building a strong cybersecurity system is much more important than incurring insurance expenses. Deep analysis revealed that cyber insurance and building a strong cyber security are very important and both should be prioritized.
- In Zimbabwe authorities still have reservations in admitting to the usage of cryptocurrency. Even though the Reserve Bank Governor once publically denounced the usage of Bitcoin the research revealed that the general public is using Bitmari a local type of Bitcoin. The finance Minister once spoke positively about Bitcoin in Zimbabwe but to date no piece of legislation has been developed to support this positive attitude.
- Further investigations revealed that some local small scale traders are trading Bitcoins on online forex trading platforms. Since locally Bitcoin has been banned most of the traders have resorted to using South African accounts.
- It is by good fortune that to date no significant cyberattacks on cryptocurrency has been reported by Zimbabwean companies despite the prevalence of Bitmari. Generally speaking no significant cyberattacks have been recorded.
- The Zimbabwean Cybersecurity systems has recently been strengthen by a Cybersecurity Bill but it still suffers on critical variables such as a deficiency of cybersecurity specialists as the few that are trained quickly move to more economically developed countries, generally speaking security is being regarded as an afterthought, and there are no insurance products designed to accommodate cyberattacks.

The Table 1 sum up the impact of blockchain to the financial services sector or monetary administrations.

Table 1. Blockchain Transformation of Financial Services

Function	Blockchain impact	Stakeholders
Authenticating Identity and Value	Verifiable and robust identities, cryptographically assured	Rating agencies, consumer data analytics, marketing, retail banking, payment card networks, Regulators
Moving Value – make a -	Transfer of value in very large and very small increments without	Retail banking, Wholesale banking, Money transfer services,

payment, transfer money, and purchase goods and services	intermediary will dramati-cally reduce cost and speed up the Payment	payment card networks, telecommunications, Regulators
Storing Value – currencies, commodities, and financial assets are stores of value, Safety deposit box, a savings account etc.	Payment mechanism with a reliable and safe store of value reduces needs for financial services; ban savings and checking accounts will become Obsolete	Retail banking, brokerages, investment banking, asset management, telecommuni-cations, Regulators
Lending value – credit card debt, mortgages, corporate bonds, municipal bonds, government bonds, asset backed securities, and other forms of credit	Debt can be issued, traded, and settled on the blockchain; increases efficiency, reduces friction, improves systemic risk. Consumers can use reputation to access loans from peers; significant for the world's unbanked and for entrepreneurs	Wholesales, Commercial, and retail banking, public finance, microlending, crowdfunding, -regulators, credit rating agencies, credit score software companies
Exchanging Value	Enhancing speed dramatically	All industries
Funding and Investing	New models	Investment banking, venture capital, legal, audit, property management, stock, exchange, Regulators
Management Risk	Lowering risk	Insurance, risk management, wholesale banking, brokerage,

		clearinghouses, regulators
Accounting for value	Dramatically improved reporting	Audit, accounting, regulators

Source: Tappsocott, D., and Tapscott, A., 2016, p. 63, adjusted.

On this foundation, The Reserve Bank of Zimbabwe proposes a blockchain and cryptocurrency based technology application model powered by a centralised cryptocurrency, i.e. CBDC with three layers to the Zimbabwean financial services sector. The three layers includes the user layer, supervisory layer and network layer. The models also describes the fundamental business processes of the central bank digital currency (CBDC's) entire lifecycle known as issuance-circulation-withdrawal in jam-packed detail. A case of Cross-border payment shall be used to explain the transaction process of central bank digital currency through the provision of theoretical guidance for CBDC design.

Central Bank Digital Currency (CBDC)
Central Bank Digital Currency is a digital expression or representation, electronic storage, and cryptographic transfer, that is encrypted for transfer of ownership. It is issued and managed by a sovereign institution such as the Central bank of Zimbabwe, subject to the financial laws and regulations in Zimbabwe. A CBDC is thus a form of centralised cryptocurrency. CBDC is another form of fiat money, similar to coin and banknote, which can be effectively exchanged for cash in denominations. The functions of CBDC includes the following:
  a) **Centralized issuance** where the central bank issues the monetary policy and provides support to the the intrinsic value.
  b) **Transferability** where the CBDC can be used as medium of monetary circulation and payment in economic activities.
  c) **Storability** of the transaction history and security of the electronic data for query, payment, exchange and management purposes.
  d) **Offline transaction** is a facility that accommodates offline transactions for a short while when the CBDC transaction is done during the moments of non-communcation with the servers, and under such circumstances the payer is not able to exchange information with other devices or systems.
  e) **Exchangeability** includes the equivalent exchange between one CBDC and other forms of the same sovereign currency, as well as the foreign exchange between CBDC and other sovereign currency.

How blockchain adds value in payments.
Blockchain is a significant technological breakthrough in decentralized cryptocurrencies permitting remote peer-to-peer value transfers amongst parties devoid of a trusted third party. The factors that blockchain may affect the development of payment industry and CBDC include:
  a) **Cost**: Blockchain-based payment systems may offer lower transaction cost than other payment methods, especially in cross-border payment, currency exchange and other payment scenarios involving multiple intermediary entities.

b) **Usability**: Compared with traditional payment methods, blockchain-based payment methods have some usability advantages, because the blockchain makes the transaction process more intuitive and easier to integrate with other services.

c) **Anonymity**: Although the blockchain itself does not provide any privacy protection, it provides an effective network architecture for anonymous payment.

Reserve Bank of Zimbabwe blockchain and cryptocurrency application technology model

This section presents a three-layered blockchain and cryptocurrency application technology model which encompasses the regulatory layer, network layer and user layer.

1) Regulatory Layer

The regulatory layer is responsible for providing control and governing mechanism of the entire life cycle of CBDC with respect to the technical and policy issues in order to ensure financial stability of the financial environment involving the CBDC. The Regulatory layer mainly includes the Reserve Bank, public key infrastructure (PKI) with identity authentication as the core, and other regulatory bodies such as sovereign institutions.

2) Network Layer

The network layer provides a bridge between the top regulators and ordinary users. The centralized tree hierarchy could help CBDC better integrate with the existing bank financial structures and facilitate the implementation of regulation.

3) User Layer

User layer comprises the low-level users and their transactions, which are not only the regulatory objects of regulatory player, but also the main data source for verification and processing of network layer.

Business process flow of the blockchain technology and centralised cryptocurrency model

The central bank, the Reserve Bank of Zimbabwe, takes full responsibility of the business process flow of CBDC throughout its entire whole life cycle, as shown on the three-layer structure of CBDC on Figure 10.

Figure 10: Three-layer structure of Central Bank Digital Currency (CBDC)

2

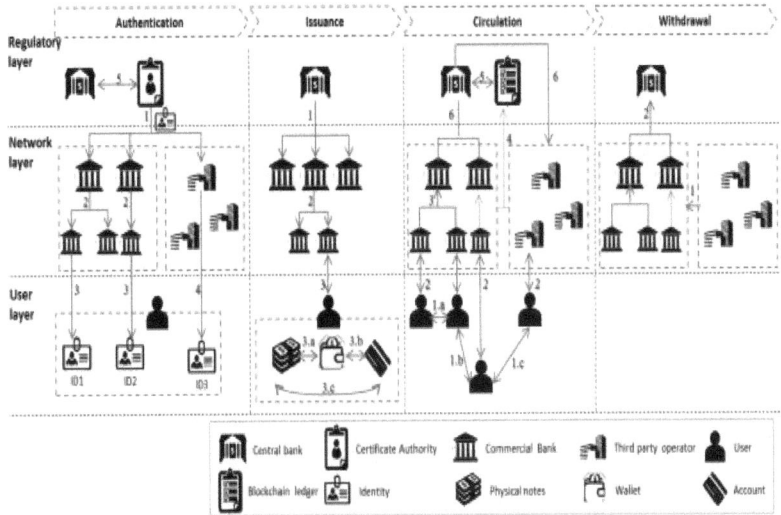

A) Identity Authentication

Legal identity authentication for the CBDC system framework must be provided to the operators. The specific business process is as follows:

1) The central bank issues the CA certificates to commercial banks and third party operators granting them legal digital identities.
2) The head offices of the commercial banks could adopt a tree-level hierarchy by sub-branching them accordingly.
3) Users can also apply for a legitimate digital identity and account address from a third-party operator that has obtained a CA certificate. The different IDs of one user are associated with the user's unique physical identity.
4) The identity information of a certain institution can be queried and verified by the central bank.

B) Currency Issuance

CBDC issuance is functionally similar to coin base transactions in Bitcoin except that CBDC is issued by a central bank or a regulatory agency authorized by a sovereign authority which follows a reasonable and legal monetary policy, while currency issuance in cryptocurrency relies on the protocols agreed in advance. A tree hierarchy structure is adopted for the CBDC issuance. The specific business process is as follows:

1. Central bank allocates CBDC to various authorized commercial banks after signature.
2. The CBDC received are assigned by the commercial banks to their branches.
3. CBDC is obtained by the users through currency exchange, withdrawal, and other means.

For the purposes of convenience of currency circulation and storage, CBDC can be stored and used in both wallet-based and account-based forms. A user can exchange physical fiat money with wallet-based CBDC, transfer of CBDC between his wallet and his account, and exchange physical fiat money with account based CBDC within the same ID. The diagram below on Figure 11 shows the application process for CBDC by commercial banks.

Figure 11: Application process for CBDC by commercial banks

Commercial Bank
Digital Currency System

Apply for
CBDC

Bank repository
receives CBDC

Central Bank
Digital Currency System

Examination
and approval

Initiate the deposit
reserve deduction

Examination
and approval

Central Bank
Accounting System

The deposit reserve is
deducted to the issuing fund

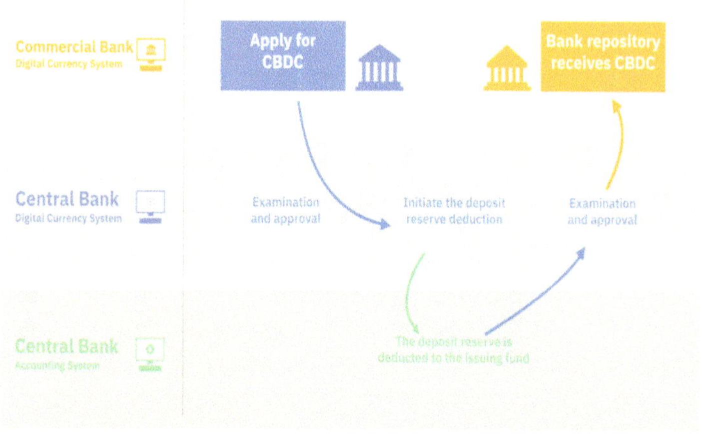

C) Currency Circulation

The circulation of CBDC mainly describes the whole business process from the user submitting the CBDC transaction to the transaction being finally recorded into blockchain ledger, which is the core functionality of CBDC. The specific business process is as follows:

1) An ID is selected by a user who then creates a transaction on a client made available by a commercial bank using that ID. The transactions users can create include:
   ❖ Inter-bank payment,
   ❖ Cross-bank payment,
   ❖ Cross-border transfer, etc.
2) The user submits a transaction to the corresponding commercial bank branch or third-party operator. Commercial banks and third-party operators are in charge for transaction verification, recording and management of account and wallet during CBDC circulation. Commercial banks and third-party operators also report back to the user the results of the transaction execution.
3) After receiving the transaction submitted by the user, the commercial bank branch verifies it and executes the anti-money laundering (AML) operations, and then submits the transaction and verification result to the upper commercial banks.
4) The verified transactions are submitted to the commercial banks and third-party operators of the blockchain network, and recorded in the blockchain ledger following a consensus protocol.
5) The blockchain ledger can be accessed by the Central bank which monitors the users' transactions.

6) Central bank also supervises all operations of commercial banks and third party operators.

D) Currency Withdrawal
CBDC withdrawal should reflect the balance of payments of banks and the prevailing economic situation as well as the functional security.

Cross-border payment by CBDC
Cross-border payment refers to the completion of value transfer across geographical boundaries through multiple fiat currencies. It is an important use case for CBDC design. It is important to provide real-time settlements and reduce costs when conducting cross-border payment in order to enable new business models, and institute new models of regulatory oversight. The payment process of the CBDC framework is explained as a use case .

i. The sender creates a transaction under an ID he owns and submits it to the corresponding bank or third party operator.
ii. Upon receiving a transaction request, the bank or third party operator performs AML operations to verify whether the transaction is in compliance.
iii. If the transaction is compliant, the bank or third-party operator locks the CBDC within the transaction.
iv. The cross-border payment smart contract begins to execute when the bank or third party operator of the sender interacts with the bank or third party operator of the receiver through blockchain network..
v. The bank or third party operator of the receiver performs AML operations to verify that the receiver and the transaction are in violation.
vi. The bank or third party operator of the receiver performs AML operations to verify that the receiver and the transaction are in violation.

The regulators are able to query, verify and recover the transaction after the transaction is over.

Implementation of the solution
To implement the proposed model, the Reserve Bank of Zimbabwe can use a programming framework known as Embark. The Embark framework is based on the concept of decentralized applications (DApps) and hence fits the technical requirements of the model. GoEthereum (geth) client, along with SolidityC programming languages can be implemented for smart contracts programming. HTML, JavaScript and Query languages can also be used to program the frontend and the GUI.

Block-chain Technology and Cyber Risks

The high level of dependency on technology has attracted the cyber criminals to target mainly the Financial Services Sector from whom they are attempting to steal valuable data, such as, personal identifiable information and financial data. As such, they are resorting to highly profitable strategies such as monetizing data access through the use of advanced ransom-ware techniques or by disrupting overall business operations through Distributed Denial of Service (DDoS) attacks.

Benefits of Block-chain technology to the Financial Services Sector

Block-chain is digital information that is stored in a public database. It usually consists of crypto-currencies and provides added security for a variety of financial transactions. There is a ledger that nobody administers. With the decentralization of ledger for payments, block-chain can provide faster payments and lower fees than banks. Block-chain affects clearance and settlement systems where distributed ledgers can reduce the costs of operations and bring more real-time transactions between financial institutions. The public blockchains now include securities such as stocks, bonds, and alternative assets. This creates more efficient capital markets.It has made it more secure to borrow money and provide lower interest rates. Trade finance has been changed with block-chain by replacing the paper heavy.

Below is the summary of the ways in which block-chain technology and crypto currency benefits the Financial Services sector:

1. **Costs Reduction** - One of the benefits of block-chain for banks is reduced costs due to reduced interaction with other third parties.
2. **Faster Transactions** - Another one of the advantages of block-chain in banking is offering faster transactions. Using block-chain technology, settlements can be increasingly optimized reducing the amount of time and money needed.
3. **Improved Security** - Shared ledgers can help banks better secure transaction information. Two security keys exist for each transaction. Rick, M.(2018) adds the use of encryption saying, where conventional financial transactions are facilitated by centralized financial institutions; however a block-chain is a decentralized system in which encrypted transactions are entered into a ledger that is shared by multiple parties.
4. **Improved Data Quality** - Modern block-chain can store any type of data and allow it to be accessed following predefined rules and regulations. By moving banking information into shared ledgers, the information then inherits the benefits of block-chain.
5. **Digital Currencies** - Banks can benefit from block-chain with the use of digital currencies. They are now able to accept digital currency to complete a variety of transactions. With crypto-currency, banks will be able to more easily clear and settle financial trades faster and more securely.
6. **Accountability** - With accountability, banks will be able to benefit from block-chain by reducing fraud and misuse of company assets. With digitally generated transactions, banks will no longer have to worry about significant errors being made. They will not have to worry about important information being fabricated with as well. Block-chain makes all transactions easy to check and verify which will, therefore, ensure that banks accurately process transactions more consistently.
7. **Compliance** - Banks will also benefit from block-chain with better compliance. They can allow auditors and government official's access to the block-chain.
8. **Reduced Error Handling and Reconciliation** – Many banks have benefited tremendously from the ease of reconciliation of transactions offered by blockchain technology. As a result, they will have the means to fix errors before they can cause a problem for the institution and their customers.
9. **Increased Transparency** - Transparency greatly increases by using smart contracts and block-chain technology. Therefore, several privacy-minded solutions have been developed.
10. **Money Transfers** - Sending money to another country is an area ready for change, and banks are already using block-chain for remittances. Consumers and businesses send hundreds of billions of dollars internationally every year, and the process has traditionally been slow, full of bureaucracy, and expensive. Bit-coin provided an "alternative" way to

move money; however, mainstream banks don't like the idea of using a volatile crypto-currency without any regulations. However, several major banks have partnered with Ripple or Stellar to facilitate cross-border payments using block-chain technology.

11. **Reduced Fraud Via Self Sovereign Identity** – Block-chain technology resists hacking, DDOS attacks, and other forms of fraud. It can also help banks and others identify individuals quickly and accurately through a block-chain-enabled digital ID.

5.0. Conclusion

The Reserve Bank of Zimbabwe analysed the functional differences between decentralized digital currency and CBDC in detail, and then give the security and functional requirements that CBDC should meet. Finally, the Bank introduced the transaction processing flow of CBDC by taking cross-border payment as an example.

The main objective of the research was achieved, it was to evaluate the performance of Cryptocurrency and Blockchain technology in a Zimbabwean cybersecurity system. Bitcoin operating on blockchain technology cannot be hacked but cyberattacks are targeting users of this platform. Zimbabwe has a weak cybersecurity system which needs serious intervention for it to work properly. Banking sector captains and executives need to band together to achieve a common goal as data extraction capabilities continue to grow. Whether its cutting costs, reducing transaction activity, or improving reliability, big data can't just benefit the end user but the industry as a whole.

Blockchain technology and big data analytics are now being implemented in various areas of the banking sector and is helping them provide better services to their internal and external customers, and also helping them to improve. Blockchain also complements data analytics technologies. Over time, blockchain technology will evolve tremendously, and the fact that central banks are also participating in research into the new technologies shows the chances of integrating blockchain technologies into the financial system across the country. Blockchain technology promises this is a safe, efficient, fast and inexpensive way to conduct transactions that will convince Zimbabweans to invest in cryptocurrencies using blockchain technology that will develop the Zimbabwean economy.

From the above discussion, blockchain may prove to be a nightmare for cybercriminals, data manipulators and others who mishandle personal data. Among the most promising is that individuals can control their own personal data (Mainelli, M., and Smith, M., 2015). Blockchain technology is not just another hype that people forget after a few days. With all its blockchain features and applications, we can safely assume that it is here to stay. All the blockchain key features are making a whole another level of impact on the web.

Recommendations

In as much as cyber threats are still low, their existence is inevitable in the near future therefore this paper has the following recommendations on the Zimbabwe:

- Local authorities should allow usage of bitcoins as they have proved to be secure, and they can ease the current liquidity challenges being faced by the nation. At the same time, the regulator should be working on a set of regulation to monitor cryptocurrency.

- Serious awareness campaigns on cybersecurity should be initiated, there is little knowledge of our cybersecurity bill such knowledge is important in enhancing the country's cybersecurity system.
- Our education system should introduce cybersecurity courses at early stages mainly because the future is digital. For the graduates, the government should come up with policies than reduce brain drain as this has harvested most of the country's specialists.
- The government should also protect its citizens by making it mandatory for most companies to have cyberinsurance. Issues to do with over dependence on a single internet provider should also be addressed in the revolution

REFERENCES

Atlam, H., and Wills, G. (2018). Technical aspects of blockchain and IoT. 10.1016/bs.adcom.2018.10.006.

Bailis, P. & Song, H. (2017). Research for Practice: Cryptocurrencies, Blockchains, and SmartContracts; Hardware for Deep Learning. Communications of the ACM, 60(5), p. 48-51.

Beck, R., and Muller-Block, C. (2017), Blockchain as Radical Innovation: A Framework for Engaging with Distributed Ledgers, IT University of Copenhagen, Proceedings of the 50th Hawaii International Conference on System Sciences, 2017, a80f5c77270bd36f1a0212bccea8651de3d4.pdf (semanticscholar.org)

Berman, D.S., Buczak, A.L., Chavis, J.S., and Corbett, C.L. (2019). "Survey of Deep Learning Methods for Cyber Security", Information 2019, 10, 122; doi:10.3390/info10040122

Bryans, D. (2014), Bitcoin and money Laundering: Mining for an Effective Solution, Inidana Law Journal, Vol 89: ISS1, Article 13 Available at https://www.repository.law.inidana.edu/ilj/vol89/iss1/13 Accessed on 13 December 2020.

Chiu, Jonathan and Koeppl, T. V. (2017), The Economics of Cryptocurrencies Bitcoin and Beyond, Queens Economics Department Working Paper No 1389.

Clinch, M. (2013). Bitcin recognizes by Germany as private Money, Accessed on 10 December 2020 from CNBC:http://www.cnbc.com/id/100971898.

Coughlan, M. Cronin, P. Ryan, F, (2007) Step by step guide to critiquing research. Part 2 Qualitative Research, British Journal of Nursing, Available on 10.12968/bjon.2007.16.11.23681 Accessed on 9 December 2020.

Crawshaw, J., and Chambers, J. (2001), A Concise Course in Advanced Level Statistics, Nelson Thornes.

Drawbaugh, K., and Temple-west, P. (2014) Bitcoins are property, not currency, IRS says regarding taxes. Accesssed on 11 December 2020 from Reuters: http://ww.reuters.com/article/2014/03/25/bitcoin-irs-idUSL1NOMM1L820140325

ECB (2012), Virtual Currency Schemes. Frankfurt: European Central Bank.

European Union Agency for Cybersecurity, (2020) Available on https://www.enisa.europa.eu/ Accessed on 5 December 2020.

Fahad, S. (2018), Blockchain Without Waste: Proof-of-Stake. Working Paper, Retrieved from https://papers.ssrn.com/sol3/papers.cfm?abstract_id3183935.

Glaser, F., Zimmermann, K., Haferkorn, M., Weber, M., and Siering, M (2014) Bitcoin-asset or currency? Revealing users hidden intentions, Tel Aviv:ECIS.

Hameed, B. I. (2020) 'Blockchain and Cryptocurrencies Technology : a survey Blockchain and Cryptocurrencies Technology : a survey', (April). doi: 10.30630/joiv.3.4.293.

Hancook, B., Ockleford, E., and Windbridge, K (2009). An Introduction to Qualitative Research, National institute of Health Research (NIHR). The NIHR RDS EM/YH

Harvey, C. (2015), Cryptofinance, Available at http://papers.ssrn.com/sol3/papers3cfm?abstract_id=2438299, Accessed on 7 December 2020

Joon, I., (2018), CoinDesk, on Centre Stage during day two of MoneyConf 2018 at the RDS Arena in Dublin. (Photo By Eóin Noonan/Sportsfile via Getty Images). Dublin , Ireland - 13 June 2018; Joon Ian Wong, Managing Director,... News Photo - Getty Images

Kabanda, G. (2020) 'Performance of Machine Learning and other Artificial Intelligence paradigms in Cybersecurity', Oriental journal of computer science and technology, 13(1), pp. 1–21. doi: 10.13005/ojcst13.01.01.

Kaushik, V. and Walsh, C, A (2019) Pragmatism as a Research Paradigm and Its Implications for Social Work Research, Social Sciences, MDPI, Open Access Journal, vol, 8(9), pages 1-17.

Kerkeni, L. et al. (2016) 'We are IntechOpen , the world ' s leading publisher of Open Access books Built by scientists , for scientists TOP 1 %', Intech, (tourism), p. 13. Available at: https://www.intechopen.com/books/advanced-biometric-technologies/liveness-detection-in-biometrics.

Kitzinger, J. (1995) Qualitative Research: Introducing Focus Groups. British Medical Journal, 311, 299-302. doi:10.1136/bmj.311.7000.299

Kshetri, N. (2017). Cybersecurity in India: Regulations, governance, institutional capacity, and market mechanisms. Asian Research Policy, 8(1), 64–76.

Manyenyere, J. (2020, July 4). Zimbabwe Awaits Its Economy To Shift To Blockchain Technology. *The Standard.*

Mainelli, M., and Smith, M. (2015), Sharing ledgers for sharing economies: an exploration of mutual distributed ledgers (aka blockchain technology). The Journal of Financial Perspectives 3 (3):38-69RoundTable. Retrieved from http://fsroundtable.org/cto-corner-what-is-a-blockchainand-

Mims, C. (2018), Why Blockchain Will Survive, Even f Bitcoin Doesn't. Wall Street Journal, Retrieved from https://www.wsj.com/articles/why-blockchain-will-survive-even-if-bitcoin-doesnt-1520769600.

Nakamoto, S, (2008), Bitcoin: A Peer-to-Peer Electronic Cash System

Nakamoto,S. (2019), Bitcoin: A Peer-to-Peer Electronic Cash System, Accessed: Feb. 23, 2019, [online]. Available: http://bitcoin.org/bitcoin.pdf, 2008.

Nyagumbo, S. (2019, May 9). Implementing a blockchain system in Zimbabwe. *Business Times.*

Piscini, E., Dalton, D. and Kehoe, L., (2017), Block-chain and Cyber Security: Lets Discuss, Deloitte EMEA Grid Block-chain Lab

Rick, M. (2018); 5 Ways Banks Can Benefit From Block-chain Technology, https://igniteoutsourcing.com/blockchain/blockchain-solutions-for-banking/, Accessed on 28/12/20

RSA, (2016). *https://www.rsa.com/.* [Online]
Available at: https://www.rsa.com/content/dam/en/white-paper/cyber-risk-appetite.pdf
[Accessed 28 Decemeber 2020].

Qin, Y. , Yuan, F. Wang, (2018), Research on the selection strategies of blockchain mining pools, IEEE Transactions on Computational Social Systems, 2018, Vol. 5, No. 3, pp.748-757.

Saunders, M. (2003). *Research methods for business.* Prentice Hall.

Schutzer, D. (2016). CTO Corner: What is a Blockchain and why is it important?

Shan., J. (2018). Blockchain; Developments and Opportunities. *Application of Blockchain technology in Banking and Finance.*

Sharma, J., (2020); Top 8 Ways Banks Benefit From Block-chain Technology, https://fintechweekly.com/magazine/articles/Top-8-Ways-Banks-Benefit-From-Blockchain-Technology, Accessed on 28/12/20

Sultan, K, Ruhi, U and Lakhani, R, (2018), Conceptualizing Block-chains: Characteristics and Applications, 11TH IADIS International Conference Information Systems 2018

Wagner, A. (2014), Digital vs Virtual Currencies. Accessed on 12 December 2020, from Bitcoinmagazine: https://bitcoinmagazine.com/15862/digital-vs-virtual-currencies/

Subramanian, R. and Chino, T (2016). The state of cryptocurrencies: Their issues and policy interactions. Journal of International Technology and Information Management, 24(3), p. 25-40

Tapscott, D. and Tapscott, A. (2016) Blockchain Revolution: How the Technology behind Bitcoin Is Changing Money, Business, and the World. Penguin, New York. https://www.amazon.com/Blockchain-Revolution-Technology

Tschorsch, F., and Scheuermann, B. (2016) Bitcoin and beyond: A technical survey on decentralized digital currencies. IEEE Communications Surveys & Tutorials 18 (3):2084-2123w hy-is-it-important//.

Tymoigne (2015), Do Cryptocurrencies Such as Bitcoin Have a Future? No: As a Currency, Bitcoins Violates All The Rules of Finance. Wall Street Journal-Eastern Edition, 265(49), p.1-2.10

Wikipedia, (2018). Blockchain, Retrieved from https://en.wikipedia.org/wiki/blockchain. Accessed on 10 December 2020.